A SMALL PREVIEW OF WHAT'S INSIDE

Cheer the F*ck Up

AN IRREVERENTLY POSITIVE ADULT COLORING BOOK

BY SASHA O'HARA

ALSO BY SASHA O'HARA

Calm the F*ck Down

IRREVERENT ADULT COLORING BOOK

Chill the F*ck Out

IRREVERENT ADULT COLORING BOOK

Happy f*cking Holidays

IRREVERENT CHRISTMAS ADULT COLORING BOOK

Calm the F*ck Down

CALENDAR & PLANNER

Cheaper than Therapy

IRREVERENTLY SNARKY ADULT COLORING JOURNAL

From the creator of the Bestseller Calm the F*ck Down

Did anyone ever tell you it's not good to brag? Well f*ck that! Give yourself a pat on the back. Own your own badass-ness. Tell the one you love how much you f*cking love them, with a little sugar and snark.

This irreverently positive coloring book will not only help you relax and unwind, it will leave you with a sense of 'Hell Yeah!' after the world has tried to have its way with you.
Cheer the F*ck Up is perfect for you if you like your self-help with a bit of sass, and your affirmations with a little piss and vinegar. It's an inappropriately awesome way to color and express the things you can't say.

Enjoy 37 beautiful and fun to color illustrations, ranging from simple to detailed in complexity. Images include mermaids, fairies, animals and abstract designs. Sayings include "Do No Harm Take No Shit", "Bite the Ass of Life", "Let's Get Weird", "Peace and Quiet. I like that shit", "Don't Damage My Calm", and many more...

Contains Adult Language. Not Intended for Children.

Dedication

This book is dedicated to those of you who are dreamers and artists at heart.

Don't let anyone tell you you're anything less than awesome.

And to everyone who colors these pages to unwind and feel better. Cheers to you!

Go rock this thing called life!

To Kas. I love you from the deepest bottom of my heart.

Thank you for being, truly, my better half.

Acknowledgements

Thank you to Caroline King for your fantastic artistic contributions and cover design for this book. You are truly gifted, and have a knack for taking what's in my head and bringing it to life. Thank you.

Caroline can be found at: shironinja.deviart.com and shiro-ninja.tumbler.com

To Autumn Pappas, you are a genuine badass of the best kind. Thank you for playing with me.

To my Promotion Team. Thank you for helping this tiny two woman business get the word out. Your input and support is so appreciated. You rock! Smooches.

To my fans. Making you happy makes me happy.

Let's Keep in Touch

If you'd like to keep in touch too, I'd love to welcome you to my Sasha O'Hara Society.

What's the Sasha O'Hara Society you ask?

It's my newsletter where you get:
1 - 4 newsletters a Month
Updates on upcoming books and projects
Exlusive contests and giveaways
Chances to vote and make your voice heard
Free downloadable coloring pages
...and more...

Sign Up at
www.sashaohara.com

My coloring books are also available as downloadable ebooks on the website!

COLOR TEST PAGE

COLOR TEST PAGE

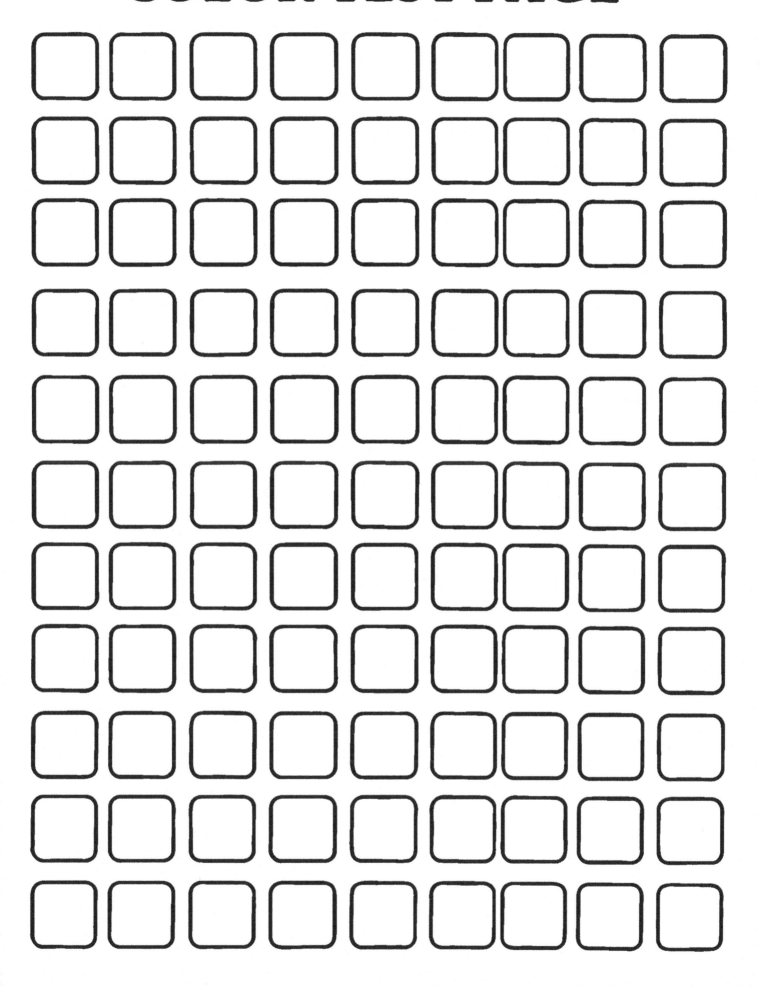

Enjoy the Shit out of this Moment

Don't Damage My Eardrum!

Be the Boss of the Life that you Create

Roses are Red, Violets are Blue, Coffee is Awesome And So am I

Classy, Sassy, and a little Smart Assy

I am one Sexy Bitch

Fuckit

Always be Yourself.

Unless you can be a mermaid,

then be a fucking mermaid.

Breathe In Excellence, Breathe Out Bullshit.

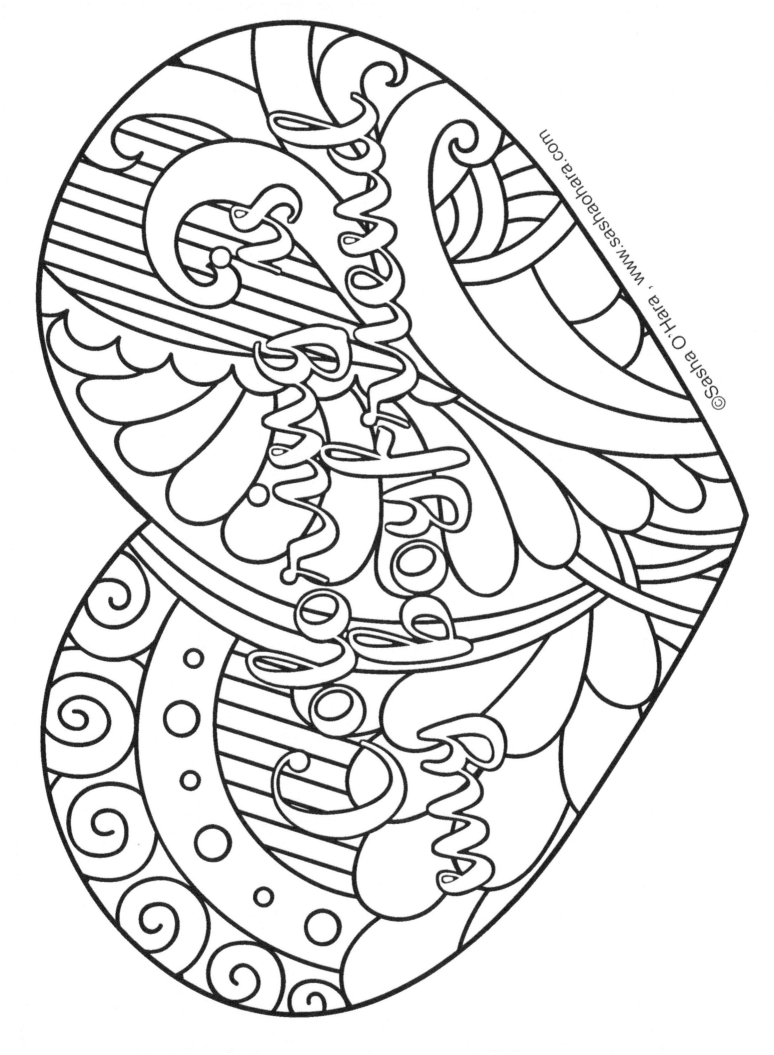

Yep

Do No Harm. Take No Shit.

I'm not a control freak. I'm a control enthusiast.

Never ever fucking underestimate this badass mofo!

I want TO GROW old and Disgusting with you

I look AWESOME naked!

Wake up and piss excellence

Hope your day is fucking magical.

Total Badass

Chase your dreams. It's good cardio.

Have a nice day, bitches.

Thanks again for purchasing this book!

There's more books to come...

If you'd like to keep in touch and be the first to hear
about them I'd love to welcome you to
the Sasha O'Hara Society

It's my Newsletter where you get
1 - 4 newsletters a month
Updates on upcoming books and projects
Exlusive Contests and Giveaways
Chances to vote and make your voice heard
Free Downloadable Coloring Pages
...and more...

Sign Up at
www.sashaohara.com

**That's also where you can find my books in
downloadable ebook format**

And keep in touch by finding me on:
Facebook at Sasha O'Hara Coloring Books
Twitter @ Sashaoharabooks
Youtube at Sasha O'Hara Coloring Books

Made in the USA
Monee, IL
07 May 2020